Super Short Scenes and Monologues

Vol. 1

Beginning

Actor

Series

Stephen Morgan

Printed in the United States of America

First Printing, 2016

ISBN 10: 0692647864

ISBN 13: 978-0692647868

Impactful Press

3940 Cypress Point

Beaumont, Texas 77707

www.ImpactfulPress.com

Ip

Impactful Press

Table of Contents

Acknowledgements

Introduction

Chapter One: How to Perform a Monologue

Chapter Two: Monologues

Chapter Three: How to Perform a Duet Scene

Chapter Four: Duet Scenes

Acknowledgements

Over the years I have had hundreds of students that inspired me every day. Most of the scenes and monologues in this book were overheard conversations about everyday situations that my students have experienced. This book is dedicated to all the students that I have had the privilege to teach. In more ways than one they have taught me to be a better teacher. This book is my way of giving back to those students and to leave a lasting legacy for future students.

Special thanks to my wife and children for allowing me to take the time to write every day.

Introduction

Every child dreams of being a superstar. Some want to be a singer or dancer, while others strive to be an actor or actress. This book is a great tool to get young actors introduced to performing monologues and duet scenes. Each monologue and scene is designed to be short and easy to memorize. Each character can be played by either a boy or girl. The content of each selection is age appropriate for young actors and provides opportunities for classwork or performance.

This book includes chapters to help understand how to perform both monologues and duet scenes. These chapters should give the young actor a better understand and tips on how to give the best performance. With all that being said I welcome you to the wonderful world of acting.

Chapter One:

How to Perform a Monologue

What is a Monologue?

If we look back to where drama came from we have to go all the way back to ancient Greece. In Greek, "mono" means alone or single and the word "logos" means to speak. By looking at what the ancient Greek words tell us we can conclude that a monologue is a speech giving by one character.

When performing a monologue we are able to look inside the character's head and see what they're thinking. Monologues can be either funny or serious. Monologues are a way to express the thoughts and feelings of a character through the use of emotions.

In the next few sections we go over some tips on how to perform a monologue.

Memorize

All monologues must be memorized. When you are performing you want your audience to believe what you are saying. If you are speaking from behind a book or paper you create a wall between you and the audience. Performing a monologue is about expressing the emotions of the character so that the audience can feel what you are feeling.

You must learn the lines well enough to say them in your sleep. You can't just think you know the lines. When it comes time to perform you have the added pressure of performing in front of an audience. That pressure can cause you to forget your lines if you are not completely prepared.

How do you memorize a monologue? The best way I have found to memorize is one line at a time. Don't try to tackle the entire selection as a whole. Memorize the first line then turn the paper over and recite the line. Then add the next line and flip the paper over and recite the first two lines. Keep adding lines as you go and after a while you will have the whole monologue memorized.

Find a Monologue You Like

A lot of people ask me, "What is a good monologue?" The answer is easy, a good monologue is one that you like and can relate to. Find a monologue that interests you and will challenge you as an actor. Your monologue must be age appropriate. If you are a middle school student you should not be performing monologues that deal with adult topics like paying bills or the struggles of being a parent.

This book is filled with monologues about "kid stuff." Find one that make you laugh or makes you cry.

Become the Character

A character is someone other than you. You must do a little research about your character. There are a lot of questions that need to be asked. There are simple questions like, how old is your character? Where do they live? What do they look like? Then you have to dig deeper into who they are. What conflicts are affecting your character? What emotion is your character feeling? How does your character interact with others? Are they nice, mean, or easily annoyed? The main question that you need to answer is what does your character want, and how are they going to get it.

Vocal Inflection

The voice is a very important tool in monologue performance. Inflection is the changing of the voice to create emotion. There are many ways we can add inflection to our performance.

The raising and lowering of the pitch is a great way to add inflection. When we get excited our voice normally goes up in pitch. When we are sad our voice tends to go lower. However you react vocally in your normal life is how you should react when acting.

The rate that we speak can add inflection. When we get excited we start to speak faster. Speaking slower may tell the audience that you are thinking about what to say. You can also add pauses for dramatic effect.

Make sure your voice matches the emotion of the character. If you are sad you would not speak really fast with a high pitch. Your speech would be in a lower tone and at a slow speed.

Using Your Body and Face

Body language when performing is divided into two parts of the body. You have above the neck which is referred to as facial expressions and below the neck which is your gestures and movement.

Facial expressions can show how a character is feeling. Your facial expressions should match the emotion in your voice. If you are happy then we should see a smile on your face and bright eyes. If your character is sad then your face should be sad. We should see a frown on your face and eyes looking down with tears in them.

Using your lower body can be tricky. There is a fine line between too much movement and not enough. Your body should tell the story without creating an interpretive dance. Think about how your character would move. How do they walk? How do they stand? Movement keeps the eyes of the audience focused on you. Unless you are an awesome speaker, if you stand still people will lose interest is your performance.

Practice, Practice, Practice

Last, but certainly not least, is practice. Practice your monologue like you are going to perform it. Just like singing or sports you should practice your acting every day. With all of these tips you are ready to jump into the world of acting.

Chapter Two:

Monologues

Jealousy

I used to think that I had nothing that anyone would be jealous of. Let's face it. I'm overweight, not very attractive and nowhere close to being rich. But then I thought of all the things that many don't have. I have a roof over my head and a warm bed to sleep at night. Yes, I might be overweight but only because I have a mother who is the best cook on Earth. I may not find myself very attractive but I have a father that sees me as perfect in his eyes. I guess I forgot that a loving family can make you feel like the richest person in the world.

Growing Up

I don't think being a grown up is all it's cut out to be. My teenage sister said just this morning, "I can't wait to be a grown up and move out." I'm scared to death about having to move out someday. Who's going to cook for me and wash my clothes? What if there is no one there to tuck me in at night? Being a grown up seems very lonely… until you get married. Then you have kids. You get to go to work and not school. That could be cool. No bedtime, no one forcing me to eat my vegetables. I guess growing up won't be that bad, but I'm in no hurry, I'll stick with the free food and mom's laundry service.

Goodbye Friend

I made a new friend last week. He has shared with me the greatest adventures of far off places. Our time together has been nothing but amazing. We spend hours together and never get bored. But today is a sad day. I just realized we will soon be apart and our journey will be ending. I guess it is true what they say. All good things must come to an end. I've prepared myself to tackle the final chapter of our adventure together. But not to worry my friend, I won't be lonely for long. I will find another book and a new friendship will begin.

Making the List

Right behind me on the wall is a list. This list could make or break my future. You have to understand the pressure I am under. My dad was the star of the football team. My mother won a state championship in volleyball. I have a lot to live up to. All I have ever wanted is to make my parents proud. They're proud of my brother. Did I mention he plays college baseball on a full scholarship? So here I am standing here about to see if I was good enough to make the list. Well here goes nothing. (turns around, then back to audience) I made the list. Not only that but I got the lead in the play. Big question now is... Will my parents be proud?

Not Mine to Give

I found it. It wasn't stolen after all. Thank God it's not broken. I can't believe you had it all this time. Did you not know how important it was to me? I wish you had taken better care of it. It looks all torn and tattered. I'm not worried. I can find someone to mend it. It may take a while but they're out there somewhere. (pause) Your right, I did give it to you, but I thought you would appreciate it more. I guess I was wrong. I realize now it wasn't mine to give, my heart belongs to God.

The Good and the Bad

We've all heard the saying, the good outweighs the bad. Not in my house. I'm a good kid, I never get in trouble. I go to church every Sunday and never complain about my chores. But I bring home one bad grade and my parents assume I'm being lazy. Did they ever stop to think that I just don't get it? It doesn't matter how hard I study I just don't understand. All I want is to make my parents proud. Why can't they see all the good that I do? I can deal with being a failure in math, but being a failure to my parents is the thing that hurts the most.

Upgraded

It is time for an upgrade. When we here that statement we get so excited about a new phone or a new car. I have decided to take that statement to mean more. It's New Year's day, the day we make resolutions for the coming year. Well my resolution is that I need an upgrade. I have decided to be the best me that I can be. I want to upgrade every part of my life in order for me to be the best. I will make a promise to myself to work harder physically, mentally, and spiritually. I want to be healthier, smarter, and grow closer to God. You better be ready world for the upgraded me 2.0.

It's Just Not Fair

I can't believe today is the last day of school. Tomorrow starts three months of sleeping till noon, watching T.V., and playing video games all night long. It's going to be so much fun. (pause) Just not for me. It's just not fair. It just so happens that I had a little too much fun in school this year and failed my English class. So instead of enjoying a relaxing summer I will be sitting in a classroom listen to the same old stuff I heard all year long. Only this time I have to actually listen to some teacher, who wants to be there less than me, ramble on about English. I language I already know by the way. I have just one bit of advice. Don't act a fool and have to go to summer school.

The Other Line

(On the phone) Yeah, I'm grounded again. My parents just don't understand what it's like to be a teenager these days. They are always riding me about being home on time and letting them know exactly where I'm at and what I'm doing. I thought this was the land of the free. Sometimes I wish they were gone so that I could live my life the way I want to live it. Hold on it's my other line. (talking to self) It's probably my parents calling to tell me they are going to be late. (clicks over) Hello. (pause) This is he/she. Who are you? (pause) The police! What do you want with me? (pause) Yes, my parents are Doug and Judy Crenshaw. (pause) What! Are they alright! (pause) They're at the St. Marks Hospital emergency room, got it. I'll be right there. (clicks back over) Jason, I have to go. My parents have been in a car wreck. (pause) I don't know if they're alright, I have to go. (hangs up phone and kneels on floor) Dear God, please don't take my mommy and daddy.

Candy Canes

It's Christmas time! This should be a time when everyone is happy. Being the new girl in school I am far from happy. Apparently there is some tradition here where everyone sends candy canes to their friends. Good news is I have no friends so I don't have to buy any candy canes to send to my friends. Bad news is that when the day comes to hand out the candy canes I won't get any. But I have a plan. The day was here. That jolly fat man was coming around to hand out those little bundles of love. When he gets to my class, he starts to call out names. Sure enough he calls out my name and hands me 5 candy canes, the most in the class. I got the look. I had arrived! Everyone was insanely jealous. Actually, I sent myself four of the five. Sadly enough, the other one was from an anonymous friend. There, you heard me. I sent myself candy canes because I have no friends. I guess I do have one friend, but I have no clue who it is.

This Is Not Camp

Mom and Dad think I need to get prepared for middle school. So guess what? They're sending me to a math and science academy. I bet you're thinking "You're kidding me right?" Oh but I only wish I was. This is my greatest nightmare, six weeks of school this summer. This is nothing short of prison. "Maybe you will meet a nice boy," my mom says. Sure, if I'm looking for someone who is creepy and pimple faced and who snorts and stares at me over their glasses. Can you say disgusting? If that wasn't bad enough, my parents also inform me that while I am gone they are going on a cruise to celebrate their anniversary. Is this a joke? While they are cruising the ocean on a luxury ship I will be learning about the ocean at nerd camp. What did I do to deserve this?

Break Up Then Break Down

All I do is sit in my room and think about what I did wrong. It's almost been a week since we broke up and I still have no clue what I could have done differently. Was there someone else? Did I say something wrong? I don't want to make the same mistakes again. I just need some answers. I really don't enjoying feeling this way. Is a person supposed to cry this much? What if my parents were right? What if we were too young and really didn't know what love is? My parents tell me "you'll get over it." They suggested finding something to occupy my time. Is it true that you never forget your first love? I hope so. But why does it have to hurt so much?

Take Time to Talk

My sister was always the pretty one, the nice one, the cool one. When I was little she was my role model. But no matter how nice I was to her, she was twice as mean to me. I loved her, but I really thought she hated me. As we got older we started to grow apart. She would ask me to do something and I would completely ignore her. We got into some of the worst fights. We would shout things to each other that we would regret. After a while, we didn't talk at all. When she left for college I thought I wouldn't miss her. My biggest regret was not telling her bye when she got in the car that day. I didn't know it would be the last time I saw her. The accident was tough on all of us but I took it the worst. If you can hear me, I love sis. Good Bye.

Unanswered Prayers

Everybody keeps telling me that things will get better, but I have a hard time believing that. My mom keeps telling me, "Everything will be alright." This is the first time I think my mom has ever lied to me. (Pause) Why does cancer even exist? Why does my dad have to be the one to have it? I spent the whole summer in the hospital with him, sitting by his bedside. He was totally drained of his color, his happiness, even his voice was gone. Every time the doctors took him away, I started to cry, not knowing if it would be the last time I saw him. Every night I prayed that God would not take my daddy away. But God knew better. He knew how much my daddy was hurting. (looking up) I'm glad you're not hurting daddy. I miss you every day.

Not Good Enough

I tried so hard this semester but still ended up with a "B" in math. Everyone knows that math isn't my strongest subject. Why can't they just accept that? My parents are always pressuring me to do above and beyond my best. Always telling me "A "B" isn't good enough! You're better than that!" I'm giving my best but I guess that's not good enough. All they see are my failures. They didn't see my science fair project that won first last year. I have an "A+" in History and English but do they ever say anything about those grades. All they see is that I am a failure in math. I know they want me to get into a really good college but I'm only in elementary school.

I Promise

I didn't even know what alcohol was until 5th grade. I didn't know how drunk people acted until about a year ago. A year ago, I came home to my dad pouring alcohol into his cup. Ever since then I haven't seen him touch water or coke or anything but his stupid alcohol. For a year, I have laid in bed listening to my mom and dad argue. I have watched my dad leave at least once a month. Not knowing when he's coming back or even where he's going. My family can't even afford to buy meals for ourselves because all of our money is spent at the liquor store. I pray my dad decides to quit before it's too late. On this day I have decided to make a promise to myself that alcohol will never have a place in my life.

History Is History

Why do you teach us about History anyway? You teach us about something that happened hundreds of years ago half way across the world. You'll spend days talking about something that happened in the 1400's. How does this have anything to do with what's going on today. Sometimes, my head is so filled with historical facts and dates that I can't even remember what year I was born in, much less the year Texas gained independence from Mexico. I mean, come on, why should we read the U.S. Constitution or the Bill of Rights when all we try to do today is figure out ways to change them. Maybe, just maybe, years from now, when time travel has been invented and we can travel back to the War of 1812, this stuff might come in handy. But until then, can we just talk about something important, like what was on TV last night?

Failure Is Not an Option

What do you mean I'm failing? There has to be a mistake. Can you check that again please? I know I did everything to make sure that I would pass. Do you know what my parents are going to do to me! I'm going to be grounded for a month! They're going to be so disappointed in me. I can't believe I let this happen. (pause) What do you mean I didn't turn in three assignments? Are you sure you're looking at the right name? (pause) WHAT! You were looking at the wrong name! It's my brother that's failing? WOW! Wait till mom hears about this. You almost gave me a heart attack. Thank you for apologizing but you are not nearly as sorry as my brother is going to be.

The Great Debate

I know this is not up for debate but I really want to go dad.
Just hear me out. There will be four teachers and at least two
parents as chaperones. I know you are concerned because it is
an overnight trip but I know that I will learn so much from
going. You told me that if I ever had the opportunity to learn
about my past I should. This is a once in a life time trip to the
National Holocaust Museum. This is a chance to see
everything that you and mom have taught me about our past.
(pause) What? You think I make a good argument for why I
should go? Does that mean you will let me go? (upset) Sure, I
guess we can go this summer as a family. That would be fun.
Just to let you know, I am growing up and someday you will
have to trust me.

The Day It All Stopped

I have to admit it, I have an addiction. For the longest time I was ashamed. Then I realized I wasn't alone. There are millions of kids out there just like me. Kids that are bound to this deadly curse we call the cell phone. I can't go ten minutes without checking for status updates or to see if anyone has liked my post. I knew it was a real problem this morning when tragedy struck. My phone had no battery. Normally this is not a huge deal but when I went to plug it in, my charger didn't work. My heart started to pound. I felt the sweat start pouring down my back. I had no answer for my dependency. I told my mom I needed a new charger now. She said, "Wait till tomorrow and we can go get you one after school." What? A whole day without my phone, I don't know if I am going to make it. It's just now lunch but I'm too sick to eat. Help me!

Work Hard For the Future

So I wrote a letter last week to my future self. I know it sounds cheesy. But when you're searching for your purpose in life it's good to have an idea of what you what your future to be like. I know, you want to know what I wrote. I can give you some highlights but most of it was private. This may shock my parents but I really don't want kids. I like kids but I don't do well with responsibility and kids are a big one. I don't want to be rich just wealthy enough to be happy. When it comes to being married am not sure. Since I don't want kids I don't have to be married but being alone doesn't sound very good. So how do I get the future I want? Desire! If I want it I have to work for it. I guess my parents were right, don't tell them I said that, hard work will pay off.

Being Average

Yesterday I went to a friend's birthday. This was the first time I had been to her house, if you can call it that. It was more like a castle. The front door was made out of iron and was at least twenty feet tall. I have to admit, when I walked in it was a bit overwhelming. Everything looked so expensive. I was afraid to touch anything. The whole house was clean and you could tell that everything had its own place. Most people would say "this is the house I want to live in someday," but not me. I love my medium sized average house. My house actual looks like people live there. It's not messy. It just feels like a home. I'm not afraid to throw my dirty clothes on the floor. Wait. Now that I think about it, it would be nice to have someone clean my room and do my chores. But until that day I'm happy being me, living in my average house with my dysfunctional family. Life is good!

Tough Decisions

Have you ever been asked a question that is impossible to answer? That's what I face right now. There are too many possible ways to answer. What if I don't make the right decision? Will it affect my entire day? Sometimes I wish someone would just decide for me. If I don't make a decision soon it will affect all those around me. I'm just going with my heart. White chocolate mocha! No wait! That will keep me up. Decaf Latte. Wait! I know I'm holding up the line. Just give me the quickest easiest thing. It's free! Thank you. (takes a drink) Black Coffee! Who drinks black coffee? At least it was free.

Thoughts on Auditioning

I'm next. Just stay calm and breath. It will all be over in two minutes. Here we go. Those lights are bright. Do I just start or wait for someone to tell me to start. I'm just going. What's the first word? Blue, right. Things are going great. I'm knocking them dead. This is the best I have ever done. Wait till my big ending. What? Thank you? But I wasn't finished. Did they not like it? Why did they stop me before the big ending? But I didn't finish! Do they know how much I want to be in this musical? Do they know that theatre is my life? This is not fair. I only got to do half of my monologue. What? Today is the singing audition? No problem! I can sing!

Unhappy Ending

Stop! Turn around and talk to me. For a month now all you have done is ignore me. I can't deal with this anymore. We used to be the best of friends. I'm sorry we broke up but that doesn't mean I don't want to still be friends. I know it's awkward for both of us but when we broke up we both said we were ok with just going back to just being friends. As far as I am concerned I still want that. I don't care that you like someone else. I'm happy for you. But I don't want to be forgotten completely. Just tell me now that you don't want to be friends anymore and we will be done. You never have to speak to me again. (pause) I didn't expect that. Ok then, that wasn't so hard. No more friendship, I'm ok with that. Now we can both move on. Good bye.

Open My Eyes

God, I need your help. This year has been horrible. New school, but not new friends. It has been so hard to get to know people. All they want to do is pick on the new kid. All I want is to be popular, like I was at my old school. I guess I should aim lower and just strive to be the kid that no one picks on. I know there are a few kids that I could become friends with but they're the kind of kids that I used to pick on myself. Nobody wants to be friends with them. (pause) Wait. I see what you're showing me. I guess this is your way God of showing me how wrong I have been. If I want to be popular, then it's time to be popular with a new crowd and for the right reason. It's better to have the right friends then no friends at all. Thank you God for opening up my eyes to all that I have done wrong. Please help me to make the right decisions.

Make Time

All week long you work hard and I appreciate that. When you get home you are exhausted and I understand. The weekend comes and all you want to do is sit on the couch and watch football and you deserve that. We use to hang out more when I was younger and I guess I out grew that. Is it my fault that you don't make time for me anymore? Did my lack of interest in the things you like cause you to ignore me? I was thinking we could hang out this weekend but it looks like I will be busy. This weekend I will say my final goodbye to you daddy. Sorry I didn't make the time.

Wake Up

Do I look like a bad kid to you? Why is it that anytime we
have an assembly at school it has to do with us not drinking,
smoking, or doing drugs? I have never even thought about
doing any of that. Why don't they focus on the real problems
in school? Like the fact that I can't walk down the hall
without someone knocking my books out of my hands? Why
does the school not pay attention to the names I'm called
everyday on social media. Just say "NO" to drugs everybody,
but say whatever you want online. If you think bullying
doesn't happen in elementary school, you're wrong. Wake up
schools!

Speaking Another Language

It's a challenge to learn a new language. Today I am accepting that challenge. I will learn the most difficult language known to man. A language that has confused students for many years. A language that most will never use but are forced to learn. Today I will learn "Algebra." I know what you are thinking, that is not a language. When they start adding letters into math then is becomes a language. If no one understands that language then it is a foreign language. I shall now begin my journey learning this new foreign language. Wish me luck!

Pretending

Have you ever pretended to be someone that you're not? Well that was the assignment. Draw a name out of the hat and be that person for a day. It was just a simple classroom experiment. One that changed my life. I drew Lily. Lily was blind. I didn't know what to do so I asked. "Tell me what it's like to be blind." She didn't say a word, instead she took a small piece of cloth from her bag and tied it around my head. The world became dark and my hearing seemed to enhance. At that point I was done pretending. That day I committed my life to help those who cannot see. I learned that a disability is not an excuse to not be able to do something but an opportunity to do it a different way.

Chapter Three:

How to Perform a Duet Scene

What is a Duet Scene?

A duet acting scene is a scene that has two characters. The scenes tell a short story and give you a glimpse of the life of the characters. In most cases the scene will have some sort of conflict that will need to be resolved. Sometimes the scene ends happily and sometimes it does not end well.

In duet acting you are able to react to the other actor through lines called "dialogue." Some people fine acting with others to be easier than doing monologue acting. Having someone to play off of is much easier for some. I would recommend starting with a duet if you are new to acting. Then after a while you can move on to monologue acting where you can pretend that the other character is there and has no lines. The following section will help you with the duet acting process.

Finding the Right Scene

When looking for a duet acting scene the most important thing to know is that you and your partner both need to like and agree on the same scene. In this book you will find that all of the duet scenes can be played by two girls, two boys, or a boy and a girl. The scenes vary from funny to

48

serious and some that are both. Now, it's time to find a partner and start acting.

Memorize

The same memorization tips on monologues that were talked about in chapter one also apply to duet acting. One thing to remember is that you are relying on someone to learn their lines and they are relying on you. Just like with monologue memorization, take it one line at a time. Take each actor's first line and read it. Then flip the script over and recite the first lines from memory. Once you have those lines add the next line for each actor. Soon you will have the lines memorized. There is a different level of acting that occurs when you no longer have the script in your hands. Work hard to get the script memorized as quickly as possible. Having your script completely memorized is called being "off book"

Know Your Character

Becoming a character and staying in that character are very important in duet acting. Look back at chapter one and review how to create a character. The character tips for performing a monologue are the same for duet acting.

Action and Reaction

Acting and reacting to what is going on in the scene is one of the most important parts of duet acting. When you are working with another character you need to react to what they are saying and doing. Your actions will cause your partner to react to you. If the other character makes you mad what is your reaction going to be? Don't just stand there waiting to say your next line. Listen to what is being said and what your partner is doing and react to them.

Body Movement and Facial Expressions

When two or more actors are on stage together there are specific movements that need to be followed. These movements are called directions or "blocking." Look back at chapter one for more tips on inflection.

Inflection

Inflections in group acting are the same as performing a monologue. Refer to the section in chapter one on inflection.

Practice, Practice, Practice

The only way to have a great performance is to practice. With monologue acting you can practice anywhere and anytime because it only involves you. With duet acting it becomes a bit more difficult. You must find a time and place for the two of you to meet and practice. It is very important to use your time wisely. You don't want to waste each other's time by not being prepared. Learn your lines ahead of time. Have a pencil to mark direction so that you can remember from one practice to the next what you have done.

Chapter Four:

Duet Scenes

Couch to Court

Mason: Come on in and have a seat.

Noah: Thanks, what do you want to do today?

Mason: Let's watch the new episode of Rebel Squirrels!

Noah: Why do I bother coming over if all you want to do is sit on the couch and watch TV?

Mason: What else is there to do?

Noah: We can go outside and play basketball.

Mason: It's too hot.

Noah: Let's ask your mom to take us to the mall.

Mason: We don't have any money.

Noah: We can just go walk around the mall.

Mason: That's pointless and involves walking.

Noah: Well I don't want to just sit here, I'm bored.

Mason: We can play a video game.

Noah: No, I want to do something active, something that requires us to get up and move around. We could both use some exercise.

Super Short Scenes and Monologues Vol. 1

Mason: What are you saying? You think I'm fat? Maybe you should just go home.

Noah: No. I'm sorry it's just that my dad has been on my case about getting out from in front of the TV and starting to getting healthier. Didn't we both say we wanted to try out for basketball when school starts?

Mason: I guess so. But I'll never make the team. Look at me. I am so out of shape.

Noah: Then let's start today and begin working out so we can get in shape. We'll do it together.

Mason: Alright, but let's start slow. Going from couch to court won't be easy.

Bad Bet

Chris: Can we talk?

Kelly: Sure, what's on your mind?

Chris: A lot actually, I have a huge problem.

Kelly: Ok, what is it?

Chris: Remember the other day when I made that bet with the guy from Westfield. I told him that our baseball team would crush them in the city championship?

Kelly: Yes, and we lost.

Chris: I know we lost and I had to pay him 20 bucks.

Kelly: So what's the problem, just pay him.

Chris: I already did. That's the problem.

Kelly: I don't understand.

Chris: I didn't have the money and he needed to be paid right away or he was going to…

Kelly: I got it. Where did you get the money?

Chris: I stole it.

Kelly: What!

Super Short Scenes and Monologues Vol. 1

Chris: I didn't really steal it, I sort of borrowed it but I plan to pay her back.

Kelly: Pay who back. What did you do?

Chris: I took the money from my mom's purse when she wasn't looking.

Kelly: That was not smart. What are going to do?

Chris: I need to put the money back right away. Any chance you got 20 dollars I can borrow?

Kelly: I wish I did, sorry.

Chris: What am I going to do?

(pause)

Kelly: Tell the truth.

Chris: What?

Kelly: Tell the truth, it is the only way to go. Yes, you are going to get in trouble but it will be worse if you try to hide it.

Chris: Your right, will you come with me? Maybe it won't be so bad if you are there with me.

Kelly: Of course, what are friends for?

Teamwork

Corey: Come on, as soon as we are done we can go back to doing our own thing.

Cameron: It's going to take hours to clean this garage.

Corey: Maybe so but the sooner we get started the sooner we can be finished.

Cameron: Doesn't dad understand that we need our rest on the weekend? School takes a lot out of us.

Corey: Stop talking and start cleaning. If we work as a team we can knock this out fast.

Cameron: I'll give you 20 bucks if you do it yourself.

Corey: Let me see the money.

Cameron: Well I don't have it yet but as soon as get 20 bucks I will give it to you.

Corey: Yeah right. Let's just get started.

Cameron: Why don't we call some friends over to help? The more the merrier and the faster we get done.

Corey: And how are you going to call your friends, dad took our phones away until we finish the job.

Cameron: I forgot. What are we going to do then?

Corey: I am going to start cleaning and hopefully you are going to help.

Cameron: There has got to be an easier way.

Corey: Look, a little hard work never hurt anyone. If I know dad he probably just wanted us to put down the video games and do something productive.

Cameron: You may be right. I have to go to the bathroom.

Corey: Sure you do.

Cameron: I will be right back, I promise.

Corey: If you are not back in five minutes then don't bother coming back, I will clean the whole thing myself. And you will owe me 20 dollars.

Cameron: Deal.

(Cameron exits)

Corey: He's not coming back. No worries, I will be 20 dollars richer and I will be sure to let dad know how productive he/she was today.

Gift Rap

Sam: Do you remember what today is?

Jordan: Sunday?

Sam: Yes, but it is also Father's Day.

Jordan: Your point?

Sam: We need to get dad a gift.

Jordan: Fine, how much money do you have?

Sam: I have just two buck. What about you?

Jordan: I got almost three. So together we don't even have five dollars to buy him gift?

Sam: I don't even think we have to buy him something. Why don't we just make something? He will love anything we give him.

Jordan: We're not kids anymore. He is going to expect us to put some thought into what we give him.

Sam: Do we just give him a cheap gift?

Jordan: No. Let's just ask mom for some money to add to what we already have.

Sam: Where do you think I got the two bucks? She gave me twenty dollars yesterday for us to go get a gift for dad.

Jordan: She didn't give me any money.

Sam: It was supposed to be for both of us.

Jordan: So why do you have just two dollars left?

Sam: Because Little Krispy's new rap CD came out yesterday and I didn't want to be the only kid in school who didn't have it.

Jordan: Are you kidding me? You bought a CD with the money mom gave you to buy our dad a father's day gift?

Sam: Yes.

Jordan: You are so selfish. Give me the CD.

Sam: Why?

Jordan: There is only one thing to do. Happy Father's day! I hope you like rap music.

Who is Leading

Adrien: Hey how's it going? Are you ready?

Skylar: Ready as I'll ever be I guess.

Adrien: Are you as nervous as I am?

Skylar: Probably more. I didn't hardly sleep last night.

Adrien: Why is that?

Skylar: I was up trying to memorize all the lines.

Adrien: I thought you already had all your lines memorized.

Skylar: I did but then I decided to try out for a different part.

Adrien: Really? What part?

Skylar: Well. The lead.

Adrien: The same part I'm auditioning for?

Skylar: Yes. Please don't be mad. I wanted more than just a chorus role. I felt like it was my turn to be in the spotlight.

Adrien: I'm not mad just a little hurt that you didn't tell me.

Skylar: You mean you wouldn't be upset if I got the lead over you.

Adrien: Not at all. But I would have studied for another part and not competed with you for this one.

Skylar: I'm sorry. I thought you would be mad.

Adrien: The only way I would be mad is if the director doesn't choose one of us for the lead.

Skylar: I agree.

Adrien: I really hope you get. You deserve it.

Skylar: Thanks for being my best friend. Will you help me with my lines before we get started?

Adrien: No, sorry I can't. You're my competition. Just kidding. Let's see what you got.

Think Before You Run

Alex: Where do you think you're going?

Peyton: What do you care?

Alex: I don't. But if mom and dad come asking me where you went I would like to give them an answer.

Peyton: Just tell them that life should be better now without me.

Alex: What are you talking about?

Peyton: I overheard mom and dad talking just now. Dad lost his job and mom is worried about paying the bills.

Alex: First of all, you should not be listening in on conversations that have nothing to do with you. Second, mom and dad will figure it out.

Peyton: This has everything to do with me. What if it doesn't work out?

Alex: How is you running away going to solve the problem.

Peyton: They said the family would have to do without somethings for a while. If I left then maybe you wouldn't have to give up anything.

Alex: That is the dumbest and nicest thing I have ever heard. So what if we have to do without for a while. We are family and family sticks together. If there is one thing I can't live without it's you.

Peyton: Thanks.

Alex: So where were you going? How were you getting there? And why do not have any clothes?

Peyton: I really didn't think that far ahead. I've never ran away before.

Alex: Obviously, Next time you run away put some thought into it. Planning is the best way to not look like an idiot. What would I do if I didn't have you here to make me look so good?

Peyton: You may act like you don't like me but I know the truth.

Alex: Whatever. Get out of my face. (pause) Hey, you don't have to run away from problems, we can face them together. I promise ever thing will be alright.

Don't Stop Believing

Taylor: Come on we are going to be late.

Shawn: I don't think I'm going.

Taylor: Why?

Shawn: I just don't feel well. Tell mom I'm just going to stay home and rest.

Taylor: You were fine ten minutes ago.

Shawn: I know but I think I just came down with something all of a sudden.

Taylor: What's going on?

Shawn: Nothing.

Taylor: Siblings can't hide things from each other, you know that. When one of us has a problem we can't hide it.

Shawn: Do you believe in God?

Taylor: Of course I do, why do you ask?

Shawn: It's just that it's hard to go to church when things have turned out the way they have.

Taylor: What do mean. Do you not believe in God anymore?

Shawn: I don't know. It's hard to believe in a God that would allow our grandmother to get sick and suffer. Why would God let our parent's divorce?

Taylor: Do you think it would be easier to go through all of this without God? I can't imagine dealing with mom and dad's divorce without God. Grandma hasn't lost her faith that she will be healed, why have you?

Shawn: But.

Taylor: But, nothing. I won't go downstairs and lie about you being sick. You can do that yourself. Now I am going to church and thank God for all the wonderful things He has blessed me with.

Shawn: I guess I'm just angry at God because of everything.

Taylor: I understand that, so pray and talk to Him. He hasn't giving up on you so don't give up on Him.

Shawn: Tell mom I will be down in a minute.

(Praying)

Shawn: Dear God, I don't know what to say other than I'm sorry.

Be the Solution

Syd: Did you see what Matthew was wearing today?

Mattie: No, what?

Syd: He has on this old jacket that he must have got from a thrift store.

Mattie: So?

Syd: So, it's ugly and has a rip in it. How can someone wear used clothes?

Mattie: It's easy, you wash it and put it on because it's all you can afford.

Syd: It's disgusting!

Mattie: It's life! Everything I'm wearing right now is used. Someone wore it before I did and I'm proud to wear second hand clothes.

Syd: I was just saying…

Mattie: You were just being rude is what you were doing. Some people don't have the luxuries that you do.

Syd: I didn't think about that.

Mattie: That's the problem. You need to think before you speak.

Syd: I'm sorry.

Mattie: Why are you apologizing to me? I'm the one who should be sorry for calling you a friend.

Syd: Wait, don't go. Tell me how to fix this.

Mattie: Instead of causing problems by saying nasty things about people, try becoming the solution by helping those people.

My Last Meal

Blake: Well, how is it?

Foster: It looks good. What is it?

Blake: It's lasagna. You haven't tasted it yet?

Foster: I was just about to. What's in it?

Blake: I'm glad you asked. In an effort to eat healthier I present to you my fat free, vegan, gluten free, low carb version of lasagna.

Foster: Wow! Where did you find the recipe?

Blake: I didn't, it is my own creation.

Foster: Shouldn't there be cheese on top?

Blake: I used a special cheese substitute made with cauliflower. It tastes almost exactly the same. Well go ahead and take a bite. I know you will love it.

Foster: Here goes. (struggles to swallow)

Blake: What do you think? You look a little green. Are you alright?

Foster: I don't know. I think I'm going to be sick.

Blake: Let me get you some water. Here drink. Is that better?

Foster: Yes, thanks.

Blake: Do you think it was my food that made you sick.

Foster: That would be my first guess. No offense but it tasted awful.

Blake: What do mean. I worked very hard on it.

Foster: Have you tasted it?

Blake: No.

Foster: So you wanted me to be your test subject?

Blake: No, I was just hoping it would turn out ok.

Foster: Taste it and tell me what you think.

Blake: No thank you. I saw what it did to you.

Foster: I need to eat something else to get this taste out of my mouth.

Blake: I made some brownies.

(gives a look)

Blake: I promise they are very unhealthy and full of sugar.

What Is It

Dakota: So what did you get me for Christmas?

Emerson: I'm not telling you.

Dakota: I will tell you what I got you.

Emerson: I don't want to know.

Dakota: If I guess will you tell me if I'm right?

Emerson: Sure, but you will never guess.

Dakota: Is it something that I can where?

Emerson: We are not going to play fifty questions?

Dakota: Well then how am I supposed to guess?

Emerson: You just have to guess without any help.

Dakota: That's impossible.

Emerson: I know that's why I agreed to tell you if you guess because you will never guess.

Dakota: Does Billy know what you got me?

Emerson: Do you think I would tell our four year brother that can't keep a secret to save his life?

Dakota: I guess not.

Emerson: And that would be pretty sad if you took advantage of a child to find out what you're getting.

Dakota: Will you tell me how much you spent? I just want to know so I can get you something that cost the same.

Emerson: I thought you already got me something. Remember, you were going to tell me what you got me if I told you what you're getting.

Dakota: Well am I going to like it?

Emerson: No, I got you something that you are going to hate in the hopes that you will never want a gift from me again. Of course you're going to like it. I put a lot of thought into what I got you this year.

Dakota: Can you at least give me a hint?

Emerson: One hint and then you are going to leave me alone. It's blue. Goodbye.

Dakota: That didn't help at all. Plan "B" where is a good hiding place for a Christmas gift.

Just What You Need

Parker: It's almost your birthday, have you decided what you are going to ask mom and dad for?

Reese: Not yet. I have made a list with quite a few things on it. It's been tough to narrow down which thing I want the most.

Parker: Let me see the list and I will help.

Reese: Here, I hope you can read my handwriting.

Parker: Alright, we can mark that one off.

Reese: Why?

Parker: You're going to be eleven. You are way too old for that. And you can take this off the list because mom already said it was too dangerous.

Reese: I know but it was worth a shot.

Parker: You already have this so let's mark that one off. We can mark all these off just because. So it looks like the one thing you should ask for isn't even on your list.

Reese: Really, what is it?

Parker: A dog! You should ask mom and dad for a dog.

Reese: But I don't want a dog. They are too much responsibility.

Parker: Sometimes it's not about you it's about the family as a whole.

Reese: So you're saying I should ask for a dog because it's what the family wants?

Parker: Exactly! You are smarter than you look.

Reese: So if I ask for a dog the whole family will help take care of it?

Parker: Sure, we will help out. It will be your dog so you will have to take on most of the responsibility.

Reese: So let me get this straight. I ask for a dog that I don't want because it is too much responsibility so that the whole family can benefit from having a dog without all the responsibilities of having to take care of it.

Parker: Right!

Reese: I think I'm going to ask for a new bike.

Parker: Why?

Reese: Because I'm smarter than I look.

Lights Out

Dylan: Will you turn that light off and go to sleep.

Ryan: Let me finish this chapter.

Dylan: No turn it off now. I can't sleep with that bright light shining in my face.

Ryan: Then roll over and it won't be in your face. This book is really getting good and I am not sleepy.

Dylan: It's way past bedtime and I'm going to tell mom.

Ryan: Mom and I have a special deal where as long as I am in bed I can read as long as I want. It's not my fault you don't like to read.

Dylan: It's not that I don't like to read, I choose not to. There are so many other things that I can spend my time doing like sleeping.

Ryan: Just admit it you don't like to read because you're no good at it.

Dylan: Just shut up.

Ryan: Are you crying?

Dylan: No, just leave me alone.

Ryan: I'm sorry that was really mean what I said.

Dylan: Your right it was. It's not my fault I don't read as well as you. You're right I am bad at reading but it doesn't mean I don't like it. I love to read. I wish I was just better at it.

Ryan: Would you be ok if I helped you read better?

Dylan: I don't know, maybe.

Ryan: Great! Let's start tomorrow. I'll turn of the light so you can sleep.

Dylan: That's alright you can leave it on. Read as long as you want. What's the book about?

Ryan: It's about a young boy who gets kidnapped by aliens and he has to find a way to escape and save the planet.

Dylan: Sounds cool! Maybe I can read it when you're done?

Ryan: You bet. Good night.

Dylan: Good night. Don't let the aliens bite.

Copy Cat

Stevie: Did you do the homework?

Pat: Yes, why?

Stevie: I forgot. Can I copy it?

Pat: I don't know if that's a good idea.

Stevie: We're best friends aren't we?

Pat: Yes but...

Stevie: But nothing, best friends let each other copy their homework.

Pat: Ok. Here you go.

Stevie: Thanks you are a life saver. If you ever forget to do your homework I will let you copy mine.

Pat: I don't think that will ever happen but thanks for the offer.

Stevie: Wow this looks hard. How long did you work on it?

Pat: That is what I was trying to tell you. I worked on this one page for almost two hours. And...

Stevie: Two hours, are you serious? I have never spent that much time on homework.

Pat: Will you let me talk?

Stevie: Hold on let me go turn this in. (comes back) Here you go thanks for letting me copy. (hand paper back) Now what were you saying?

Pat: I was trying to tell you that the reason it took so long was that I had no clue what I was doing. Mrs. Jones told me not to turn it in this morning. She wants me to come after school so she can help me with it. Every answer on that paper was wrong.

Stevie: You mean I'm going to get a zero anyways.

Pat: It looks that way. Sorry, I was trying to tell you.

Stevie: That's alright. That's what I get for cheating.

Pat: Looks like you may be in more trouble. I think Mrs. Jones wants to see you.

Stevie: Awe man!

Pat: Good Luck!

Don't Move

Tracy: Come on. Open the door already.

Lynn: No, I'm so mad at you.

Tracy: This is silly, open the door now. It's cold out here.

Lynn: Good, maybe you will think before you lie to me.

Tracy: I didn't lie. I just didn't tell you the whole truth.

Lynn: Well best friends don't withhold vital information that could change our lives forever.

Tracy: I don't see what the big deal is. I thought you already knew.

Lynn: How would I have known? Who else have you told that could have possibly shared this information with me?

Tracy: Nobody, you are the first one that I have told. I just found out yesterday.

Lynn: Then how would I have known?

Tracy: I don't know. Please open the door so we can talk.

(opens the door)

Lynn: Go on. Explain everything.

Tracy: OK. My dad's boss decided to give him a raise. The raise means a new position at a new location. We have to move immediately.

Lynn: This isn't fair we have been best friends since kindergarten. Who am I supposed to start middle school with next year?

Tracy: Can I please come in, I'm freezing.

Lynn: Yes, sorry. Come on in.

Tracy: Thanks. (long pause) We can still call and talk.

Lynn: You promise, every day?

Tracy: Yes, I promise.

Lynn: Where are you moving to?

Tracy: Grand Lakes.

Lynn: Grand Lakes? That's only like twenty minutes away?

Tracy: Really? I thought it was farther.

Lynn: We may not be in the same school but we can still get together on the weekends and holidays.

Tracy: Best friends forever?

Lynn: Best friends forever.

Don't Be a Chicken

Alex: Did you hear that?

Lonnie: I think so. What do you think it was?

Alex: I don't know but I'm ready to go home.

Lonnie: Just a few more hours and then we will be legendary.

Alex: Tell me again how spending the night in a cemetery is going to make us legendary.

Lonnie: Everyone will know that we fear nothing after tonight.

Alex: But that's not true. I fear lots of things, especially strange noises that could eat me.

Lonnie: Nothing is going to eat you.

Alex: How do you know?

Lonnie: Because the dead don't eat.

Alex: That's not funny. Can we please just go?

Lonnie: If we are not seen leaving the cemetery when the sun comes up everyone will know that we chickened out.

Alex: I'm ok with being a chicken, really I am.

Super Short Scenes and Monologues Vol. 1

Lonnie: Why don't you try to sleep? I will stay awake and keep an eye out for ghosts.

Alex: Again, not funny. Wake me up if you see anything.

Lonnie: You got it. Sleep tight.

Alex: Fat chance. I wish I knew how to sleep with one eye open.

Lonnie: Just shut up and go to sleep. You got a nice spot right here on Mr. Martin's grave.

Alex: What did you say? Whose grave am I sleeping on?

Lonnie: Mr. Alex Martin.

Alex: That's my name.

Lonnie: It's just a coincidence. There are a lot of Alex Martin's.

Alex: I don't believe in coincidences. I'm out of here.

Lonnie: Hey, don't be a chicken. Ok, I'll be a chicken too. Wait up!

83

Wear What You Feel

Tanner: What are you doing? You are going to get in so much trouble.

Sean: I am practicing my right to freedom of speech.

Tanner: But that shirt is not in dress code. You are going to get sent home.

Sean: Let them try to send me home. We have the right to wear whatever we want and no one can tell us differently.

Tanner: Actually they can. At the first of the year we signed a contract that said we would follow all the rules of the school or there would be consequences. The dress code is part of the contract that you signed.

Sean: A minor cannot legally sign a contract.

Tanner: Your parents also signed it saying that you would follow the rules. Does your mom know you wore that?

Sean: Not really. I changed in the bathroom when I got here.

Tanner: What is wrong with you? Do you want to get grounded?

Sean: I don't care. It's time we take a stand for what we believe in. No more dress code.

Tanner: There are better ways to go about doing away with the dress code.

Sean: Like what?

Tanner: You could have the students sign a petition. Or set up a meeting with student council so that your voice can be heard. Breaking the rules is not the way to go.

Sean: Maybe you're right. Do you think any teachers have seen me yet?

Tanner: I don't think so. If you can make back to the bathroom without being seen you can change back into your uniform.

Sean: Walk in front of me in the hall so that no one sees me.

Tanner: Here just take my jacket. Hurry, first period is about to start. You don't want a tardy. Unless you are trying to break the rules and get detention. Just kidding, hurry.

Ice Cream and Popsicles

Sammy: So what did the doctor say?

Andy: It's not good. I have to have an operation.

Sammy: What for?

Andy: They have to remove my tonsils.

Sammy: Oh, that's no big deal. My sister had that done last year.

Andy: Really, does it hurt?

Sammy: Maybe a little after you wake up.

Andy: What do you mean wake up?

Sammy: They put you to sleep so you don't feel anything during the operation. Then they wake you up.

Andy: Ok. So you don't feel them do the operation but after you wake up it hurts?

Sammy: I little. My sister said it was like having a really bad sore throat.

Andy: I don't like having a sore throat.

Sammy: The good news is she got to eat all the ice cream and popsicles she wanted. Only because that was all she was able to eat.

Andy: I can get use to that. Did she have to miss any school?

Sammy: Just a day or two.

Andy: Sweet! Two days off from school sitting on the couch watching cartoons and eating ice cream and popsicles!

Sammy: When you put it that way, you are so lucky you get to have an operation.

Andy: I guess I was blessed with bad tonsils. Can I ask you a stupid question?

Sammy: Sure, anything.

Andy: What is a tonsil?

Sammy: I have no idea.

Is He Real

Charlie: Can you play after school today?

Dylan: No, I got grounded again.

Charlie: What did you do this time?

Dylan: I told my little brother that Santa wasn't real.

Charlie: Why would you do a thing like that? That was mean.

Dylan: I know but he was annoying me. I just wanted him to leave me alone.

Charlie: What makes you think Santa isn't real?

Dylan: Are you serious?

Charlie: When did you stop believing?

Dylan: I guess when I was about eight.

Charlie: What lead you to stop believing? Did someone tell you he wasn't real?

Dylan: No, it's just that it was kids' stuff. For years I would set out cookies and milk and wait up to catch a peek of him but I never did.

Charlie: So you stopped believing in Santa because you never saw him? Do you ever see results from him visiting your house?

Dylan: What do you mean?

Charlie: Did he leave you presents?

Dylan: Sure. Lots of presents.

Charlie: Well I for one would not stop believing in Santa if he is still bringing me gift. I was always told that when I stop believing the gifts would stop.

Dylan: You mean you still believe in Santa?

Charlie: I sure do, and I have never seen him in person.

Dylan: I think that's silly.

Charlie: What, to believe in someone you have never seen. I believe in Jesus and I have never seen him.

Dylan: That's different.

Charlie: How is it different? God's spirit lives within us and makes us happy. Do you want to know why adults are always so unhappy? They stopped believing and lost the Christmas spirit. They lost their joy.

Dylan: I get it now. I've got to home and talk to my brother. Bye.

Bad Influence

Ashton: You know this is all your fault.

Casey: Why is it my fault? You're the one that started talking to me.

Ashton: I was just asking you a question about the assignment.

Casey: Then why didn't you tell the teacher that. Maybe we wouldn't be sitting here in detention.

Ashton: I tried but she just wouldn't listen. She never has liked me.

Casey: Well thanks to you she doesn't like me now. My mom is going to kill me when she finds out I got in trouble.

Ashton: Just blame it on me. Your mom already hates me.

Casey: Your right she does. What you don't understand is that if I blame this on you then she will forbid me from hanging out with you forever.

Ashton: You mean she won't let you be my friend anymore?

Casey: That's right. I won't be allowed to go to your house and you can't come to mine. We won't even be able to hang out at school.

Ashton: She can't do that. How is she going to know if we hang out?

Casey: Believe me she as her ways of knowing. Plus she's right. You are always getting me in trouble.

Ashton: Well I'm so sorry I'm such a bad influence on you. Don't worry about me getting you in trouble anymore.

Casey: What do mean.

Ashton: I will save you and your mom the trouble of forbidding me to hang out with you. We are no longer friends.

Casey: Is that really what you want?

Ashton: No, but real friends do whatever they can to protect their friends. If I'm messing up your life then it's time for me to end our friendship. As soon as we get out of here you never have to see me again.

Casey: You're over reacting.

Ashton: Detention is over. Time to find a friend who I'm not a bad influence on. Maybe their mom won't hate me. Goodbye.

Take Note

Jodie: Hey, I think you better see this.

Terry: What is it?

Jodie: Just look.

Terry: I don't understand. Who would write something like this?

Jodie: I don't know. I found it on the floor in the hallway. Somebody must have dropped it. What are you going to do?

Terry: I don't know. What would you do if someone wrote a bunch of nasty things about you in a note?

Jodie: I guess I would tell the principal. But we don't have a full name of who wrote it. That is the first thing he is going to ask is who wrote the note.

Terry: Well then how do we find out who wrote it? I have a good idea of who wrote it but no way to prove it.

Jodie: It's just signed with the initials H. K. There can't be that many students in the school with those initials.

Terry: I have my yearbook with me. We can go through each grade and make a list of students with those initials.

Jodie: Good idea. Then we can confront each of those students and find out who wrote it.

Terry: Don't you think that may cause some trouble? Blaming innocent people until you find the one who did it. Even when you do find the person they already don't like you. I don't want to see you get in a fight.

Jodie: Maybe you're right. Once we have the list we can take it to the principal and let him figure out who wrote it.

Terry: Why are people so mean?

Jodie: I don't know. They're cowards. It's so easy to write something bad about someone in a note. If you have something to say then say it to my face.

Terry: You're right. Come on let's start working on that list.

Very Rewarding

Randy: I'll race you home.

Leslie: You're on! Hey look, a wallet.

Randy: Pick it up.

Leslie: You pick it up.

Randy: Whatever, chicken!

Leslie: Open it. Is there any money?

Randy: Calm down. Whoa! There is like two hundred dollars in here.

Leslie: Sweet! Take the money and put the wallet back.

Randy: I don't know if we should do that.

Leslie: Why not? Finder's keeps, loser's weepers.

Randy: Grow up. There are credit cards in here. I know when my mom lost her purse last year it was a nightmare having to cancel all her credit cards.

Leslie: So what should we do?

Randy: Find out who it belongs to and return it to them. They might even give us a reward.

Leslie: I never thought about that. Ok, so how do we find them?

Randy: Let's use our detective skills here. There are pictures. We can ask around if anyone recognizes anyone in the pictures.

Leslie: Wait! Here is a library card. We can go to the library and see if they can look up the account and give us an address.

Randy: You are a genius! Let's go!

Leslie: Wait. What if we just take the money out and say we found it with no money inside?

Randy: I'm not comfortable being dishonest. What if that is all the money they have to live on for the whole month?

Leslie: You're right. It is crazy how money can make a person become insane. I'm glad you're thinking straight. To the library!

Making Friends

Jerry: Have you met the new kid?

Mickey: He's in my math class, kind of strange if you ask me.

Jerry: I thought he was nice. I was going to ask him if he wanted to come over after school and play video games or something.

Mickey: Why would you do that? He's weird and kids will talk about you if you start being buddies with him.

Jerry: What's so weird about him?

Mickey: He's one of those book nerds and reads all the time. And he has no friends.

Jerry: He just moved here! How do you expect him to have friends yet?

Mickey: I don't know, maybe if he would pull his nose out from those books and talk to people they would like him.

Jerry: Maybe he has his nose in books because he is too shy and is waiting for someone to talk to him.

Mickey: Well you can be that guy then, not me!

Jerry: Can I tell you a story?

Mickey: Sure.

Jerry: Remember your first day at this school? At lunch you were sitting under a tree eating by yourself. Then what happen?

Mickey: You came over and ate with me.

Jerry: That's right. It was my goal that day to make a new friend. A friend I've had for five years now. Do you remember what you were doing while you were eating?

Mickey: No, I don't remember.

Jerry: I do! You were reading a book. That's right! You had your nose in book. But I was determined to make a friend.

Mickey: Thanks for coming over and talking to me. I guess I was just being close minded to the idea of making a new friend.

Jerry: It's scary to walk up to someone and start talking. But it's easier when you can do it with a friend.

Mickey: You're right! Let's go find the new kids and get to know him.

Jerry: Lead the way my friend.

After the Dance

Angel: Wow it feels so good out here.

Brice: Yes it does. The perfect weather to end the perfect night.

Angel: I would have to agree. This was the best school dance ever.

Brice: Only because you didn't stop dancing all night long. How many people did you dance with tonight?

Angel: Too many to count. What about you and your dance partner. Must have been nice to dance with the same person all night long?

Brice: I have to admit it was pretty nice. I think we made a real connection.

Angel: What time is your mom picking us up?

Brice: What do mean? I thought your mom was picking us up.

Angel: Aren't we spending the night at your house?

Brice: Yes but your mom was supposed to pick us up and take us to my house.

Angel: So we have no ride home. Let's go back in and call someone.

Brice: Wait. Who do you want to call?

Angel: We have to call your mom because my mom is out of town.

Brice: I was just about say that my mom is not available. She is at an office party and I know she won't be home till late. She told me that we could make whatever we wanted for dinner and she would be home later.

Angel: Let's just go back in and see if someone can give us a ride.

Brice: You're not going to believe this, the door is locked.

Angel: Are you serious? What do we do now?

Brice: I don't have a clue.

Angel: I guess we could walk.

Brice: It's like five miles.

Angel: Then what's your solution.

Brice: I guess we're walking. At least it's good weather.

Angel: Was that a rain drop?

Brice: You have got to be kidding me.

Angel: Let's just walk fast.

Not My Fault

Chris: What did you do this time?

Tyler: What makes you think I did something?

Chris: You are sitting outside the principal's office and you look like your dog just died.

Tyler: Just leave me alone.

Chris: Sorry, didn't mean to bother you.

Tyler: Wait! It wasn't my fault! She was talking to me and I was just answering her.

Chris: So you got in trouble for talking in class? Your parents are not going to be happy.

Tyler: Tell me about it. I'm going to be grounded for a month. Worst part is that it wasn't even my fault.

Chris: Just tell the principal what you told me. You were just answering a question.

Tyler: It won't do any good. I was the one caught talking. I'm always the one who gets caught doing something wrong.

Chris: Why are you giving up so easily?

Tyler: I'm the bad kid. The principal knows it, the teachers know it, you even know it. I did the crime I will do the time.

Chris: But it wasn't your fault this time.

Tyler: Exactly, this time it wasn't my fault. I've messed up too many times. It doesn't matter. I am who I am.

Chris: What you are is my friend and I am going to help you.

Tyler: How?

Chris: I'm going to go in with you and talk to the principal.

Tyler: It won't work.

Chris: Maybe not, but you are my friend and I'm going to try. Let's go.

Tyler: What are you going to say?

Chris: I'm going to tell him how awesome you are and that if teachers would start treating you like a good kid then maybe you would act better.

Tyler: Thanks.

Chris: No problem.

The Sub

Cory: Did you hear the good news?

Blake: No, what?

Cory: We have a sub today in Miss Harvey's class.

Blake: Sweet, a substitute. This is going to be a great day.

Cory: Depends on who the sub is. The wrong sub could make our day miserable. Do you know who it is?

Blake: Nope, but whoever it is they better be ready for me.

Cory: What evil things are you planning for today?

Blake: Let's just say this may be the last time they sub at this school.

Cory: Wow, what are you going to do?

Blake: I think I will just let it be a surprise.

Cory: Whatever you are up to please leave me out. I can't afford to get in trouble again.

Blake: Who is that?

Cory: I have no clue but he is huge. Does he realize this is a school and not the gym?

Blake: I don't think he is here to workout. I hope he's not our sub.

Cory: Awe man, he just went in our classroom. So much for a fun day.

Blake: I don't know. We could still have a little fun.

Cory: Are you crazy? That guy could eat you for lunch. He will crush you if you mess with him.

Blake: Maybe you're right. Let's just get through this horrible day and pray that Miss Harvey is back tomorrow.

Food For Thought

Bailey: That looks good!

Cam: It is, and it's mine.

Bailey: I didn't say I wanted any. I just said it looked good. I'm just trying to have a conversation.

Cam: Well just in case you were thinking about wanting some, I'm not sharing.

Bailey: Why are you being so mean today?

Cam: I'm just hungry and don't want to share. Just leave me alone.

Bailey: Fine, I'll go sit somewhere else.

Cam: No, wait! Never mind, go.

Bailey: Tell me what's going on, talk to me.

Cam: It's kind of personal and a little embarrassing.

Bailey: I'm your friend. I won't say anything. What's up?

Cam: My dad lost his job yesterday.

Bailey: No way! Sorry to hear that.

Super Short Scenes and Monologues Vol. 1

Cam: Until he finds another job my family has to be careful how we spend money.

Bailey: I understand.

Cam: Sorry for being so protective of my lunch but I didn't eat well yesterday and I was just hungry.

Bailey: Here take half of my sandwich.

Cam: No, that's ok you eat it.

Bailey: Why don't you come over to my house after school for dinner? My mom is making meatloaf.

Cam: That would be great. I love meatloaf!

Bailey: We always have a lot left over if you want to take some home to your family.

Cam: That would be nice. Thanks.

Bailey: You sure you don't want half of my peanut butter and tuna sandwich.

Cam: I don't think I will ever be that hungry.

Unknown Results

Len: Hey, where have you been? I haven't seen you all week.

Terri: I just wasn't feeling well.

Len: Oh, did you have the flu or something?

Terri: Yeah, something like that.

Len: Do you want to come over and play today?

Terri: No thanks, I have a lot of homework to catch up on.

Len: Ok, if you change your mind just let me know. I'll see you at lunch.

Terri: I think I'm going to skip lunch today so I guess I'll just see you tomorrow.

Len: You, skip lunch, that doesn't sound like you. Are you sure you're ok?

Terri: Yeah, just not hungry. (pause) I'm sorry, I can't lie to you. You're my best friend. I've been in the hospital the past few days.

Len: Oh no, what's wrong?

Terri: That's the thing, they don't know.

Len: What's been going on?

Terri: I've just been really tired and haven't really wanted to eat much. My mom took me to the doctor a few days ago and he put me in the hospital to run some tests.

Len: So when do you find out what the tests says?

Terri: Today. I'm so scared.

Len: Why don't you go home, you don't need to be here?

Terri: I want to be here so that I can have something to take my mind off of waiting.

Len: Well then let's stop talking about it and do something else. Today after school I will be with you until you find out the results.

Terri: Thanks.

Len: That's what friends are for.

www.ingramcontent.com/pod-product-compliance
Lightning Source LLC
Chambersburg PA
CBHW071013040426
42443CB00007B/749